YOUR KNOWLEDGE HAS VALUE

- We will publish your bachelor's and master's thesis, essays and papers

- Your own eBook and book - sold worldwide in all relevant shops

- Earn money with each sale

Upload your text at www.GRIN.com
and publish for free

Bibliographic information published by the German National Library:

The German National Library lists this publication in the National Bibliography; detailed bibliographic data are available on the Internet at http://dnb.dnb.de .

Imprint:

Copyright © 2018 GRIN Verlag
Print and binding: Books on Demand GmbH, Norderstedt Germany
ISBN: 9783668829336

This book at GRIN:

https://www.grin.com/document/448213

John Uzo

A Bargain Model for an E-Commerce Platform

GRIN Verlag

GRIN - Your knowledge has value

Since its foundation in 1998, GRIN has specialized in publishing academic texts by students, college teachers and other academics as e-book and printed book. The website www.grin.com is an ideal platform for presenting term papers, final papers, scientific essays, dissertations and specialist books.

Visit us on the internet:

http://www.grin.com/

http://www.facebook.com/grincom

http://www.twitter.com/grin_com

BARGAIN MODEL FOR AN ECOMMERCE MODEL

BY

JOHN U. UZO

A PROJECT REPORT SUBMITTED TO THE DEPARTMENT OF COMPUTER SCIENCES, UNIVERSITY OF LAGOS, IN *PARTIAL FULFILMENT OF THE REQUIREMENTS FOR THE AWARD OF THE DEGREE OF* MASTER OF INFORMATION TECHNOLOGY (MIT)

DECEMBER, 2017

DEDICATION

This work is dedicated to God who helped me complete it despite all adversity.

ACKNOWLEDGEMENTS

I would like to acknowledge my supervisor, Dr. Victor Odumuyiwa for his patience and encouragement. I would also like to acknowledge Yihua Sheng's for his extensive work on dynamic pricing. Though I have not met him in person, but I hope to. I would also like to acknowledge Gbolahan Okerayi for his immense assistance on the development of the system with such short notice.

ABSTRACT

Bargain model is arguably the most underachieving model of all ebusiness model. However, bargaining (haggling or bartering) in markets have existed since the inception of trading itself, as early as the trade-by-barter era. In this paper, a system is built to simulate this behaviour between buyer and seller and to show that it is enjoyable, practical and certainly a valuable commercial product. The bargain model has some advantages over fixed pricing, which could be exploited to the benefit of sellers, and buyers alike. The software system designed and implemented in this work is essentially a web app, achieved using objected-oriented programming; using languages and tools such as Python, Django, HTML, SASS, JavaScript, Postgres and agile methodology.

iv

TABLE OF CONTENTS

DEDICATION ii

ACKNOWLEDGEMENTS iii

ABSTRACT iv

TABLE OF CONTENTS v

LIST OF FIGURES vii

INTRODUCTION 1

1.1   Overview 1

1.2   Problem Definition 1

1.3   Aim and Objectives 2

1.4   Scope of Study 2

1.5   Methodology 2

1.6   Significance of Study 2

CHAPTER TWO 3

LITERATURE REVIEW 3

2.1   Introduction 3

2.2   Electronic commerce 4

2.3   E-business models 4

2.4   Bargain model per se 6

2.5   Yihua Philip Sheng's work 8

CHAPTER THREE 10

SYSTEM ANALYSIS AND DESIGN 10

3.1   Overview 10

3.2   Requirements analysis 11

3.2.1   Requirements elicitation 11

3.2.1.1   Functional requirements 11

3.2.1.2   Non-functional requirements 12

3.2.2   System Requirements Analysis 12

3.3   Use Case Analysis 13

3.3.1   Background 13

3.3.2   Use Case Diagram 15

3.3.3   Use Case 16

3.4   Activity Diagram 24

3.5   Class Diagram 25

3.6   Class Diagram (Detailed) 26

3.7   Communication diagram 26

3.8   Behaviour State Diagram 27

3.9   E-R Diagram 28

3.10   Data Storage Design 28

3.11   User Interface 32

CHAPTER FOUR 35

IMPLEMENTATION 35

4.1   Introduction 35

4.2   Software components 37

4.3   Testing 39

CHAPTER FIVE 40

CONCLUSION AND RECOMMENDATION 40

5.1   Summary 40

5.2   Advantages and Opportunities 40

5.3   Problems Encountered 41

5.4   Recommendations 42

5.5   Conclusion 42

REFERENCES 44

LIST OF FIGURES

Figure 1 - Price change strategy (Sheng, 2004) 9
Figure 2 - Use case diagram 16
Figure 3 - Activity diagram 24
Figure 4 - Class diagram 25
Figure 5 - Sequence diagram 25
Figure 6 - Detailed class diagram 26
Figure 7 - Communication diagram 27
Figure 8 - State machine 27
Figure 9 - E-R Diagram 28
Figure 10 – User Interface Login 32
Figure 11 - User Interface - My products 32
Figure 12- User Interface - Set price 33
Figure 13 - User Interface - New offer 33
Figure 14 - User Interface - All products 34
Figure 15 - User Interface - Make an offer 34
Figure 16 - Home page 37
Figure 17 - Login page 37
Figure 18 - Admin page 38
Figure 19 - Admin page - User profile 38
Figure 20 - Dynamic pricing (source: Virgillito, 2016) 41

CHAPTER ONE

INTRODUCTION

1.1   Overview

Information Communication Technology (ICT) is a beautiful gift to humanity. Since its birth in the 1950s, it has been helping humanity to solve life's problems. Information Technology, as it is often called, owes its growth to the inception of the modern computer. Great things must be either discovered or invented, and it takes great minds to take on this task, usually sacrificing life's pleasures to answer question that are posed to the human race. Notable individuals in computer science include Charles Babbage, who is known as the father of computers (Azeez, 2016). Jon von Neumann and Alan Turing are also names synonymous with the birth of the computer, hence the digital age.

Electronic commerce (ecommerce for short), is a branch of information technology which has seen tremendous growth over the last couple of decades. It is basically the exchange of goods and services over computer networks. There are so many successful models of ecommerce, which include business to business, business to consumer, consumer to consumer, portal model and auction model.

1.2   Problem Definition

Most, if not all ecommerce models known to man, have been tried out in cyberspace, and a majority of them have been successful. However, there is one model which is yet to be employed. It is called the bargain model. Sadly, there is not enough data to confirm the reason for this. But from observation, one can speculate that these factors may have a contributing influence for this phenomenon.

  i.   It takes a longer time to reach a deal.
 ii.   It is computationally demanding
iii.   It is not traditionally popular with Americans, hence Silicon Valley would not bother about it.
 iv.   There is so much focus on fixed pricing and auction pricing already.

1

1.3   Aim and Objectives

The aim of this paper is to build a bargain style ecommerce platform that allows a buyer and seller to engage in negotiations over the price (and other features) of a product.

The aim is achieved by building a web app which allows users to connect as either buyer or seller using a web browser via the internet. The paper also reviews research done by authorities in the ecommerce field on dynamic pricing (bargain model is a type of dynamic pricing). A simple system is designed here to show that this concept is not only possible, but makes practical sense as well as enjoyable. It certainly has its benefits, hence, it is worth the study.

1.4   Scope of Study

Even though the study is on ecommerce, because so much work is already available on ecommerce, the paper will focus on the bargain aspect of ecommerce. This is because, there is not one difference between any other type of ecommerce from the bargain model safe that it uses a different marketing strategy to attain sales.

1.5   Methodology

The system is essentially a web app. The paper describes the full software development life cycle (SDLC) for the system. However, because further research and development on this model will be carried out building on the basis of this paper, there will be some highlights of the proposed, more practical system.

Because of the beauty of object-oriented programming, requirement analysis all through maintenance will be conducted using object-oriented technology. Agile development is will be utilised to develop the best possible software for this concept.

1.6   Significance of Study

The importance of this research could be immense. The onlooker will immediately espy that it has an appealing economic importance. A business concept paper, a business plan and a presentation will naturally follow this document.

CHAPTER TWO

LITERATURE REVIEW

2.1   Introduction

Having seen the successes of Amazon^{TM}, Facebook^{TM}, Instagram^{TM}, Alibaba^{TM}, WhatsApp^{TM}, Google^{TM}, Apple^{TM}, IBM and Dell, it is a no-brainer that every millennial child is thinking of how to cash in on this new trend of cash spinning ventures – well, at least, for ambitious kids. Information Technology involves the conversion of data to information, the dissemination of these data and information, the processing and manipulation of these data, its movement to and fro, and an all round beneficial use of information using computer systems.

Azeez (2017) gives us several definitions for information technology (IT) – I will enumerate them thus:

"Information Technology is the application of computers and telecommunication equipment to store, retrieve, transmit and manipulate data, often in the context of a business or other enterprises".

"The application of science, especially to industrial or commercial objectives on the processed data (information)".

"Information Technology (IT) is a technology which uses computers to gather, process, store, protect, and transfer information".

"ICTs are the hardware and software that enable society to create, collect, consolidate and communicate information in multimedia formats and for various purposes".

And finally he quote Ptmsinform (2013) saying, "Information Technology (IT) is the study, design, development, implementation, support or management of computer-based information systems, particularly software applications, computer hardware and mobile devices".

After the dot com bubble, people are now giving information technology more respect, as not just a wave or a niche, but a field of its own. It goes without saying that we are in the digital age, where there is more focus in making systems and products digitally compatible.

2.2   Electronic commerce

A branch of information technology, electronic commerce, or e-commerce (also ecommerce) for short, has been thriving lately. To understand ecommerce, a brief introduction to e-business (electronic business, ebusiness) will be made. Adewole (2017) explains e-business to be "the integration, within the company, of tools based on information and communication technologies (generally referred to as business software) to improve their functioning in order to create value for the enterprise, its clients, and its partners". Adewole (2017 p.59) continues by distinguishing ecommerce from ebusiness, stating that "e-commerce involves digitally enabled commercial transactions between and among organizations and individuals".

2.3   E-business models

"A business model can be defined as the organisation of product, service and information flows, and the sources of revenues and benefits for suppliers and customers. An e-business model is the adaptation of an organisation's business model to the internet economy" (Combe, 2006).

Business to Consumer (B2C) – This model stems from the idea where businesses deal directly with their customers using an ecommerce platform. There are many examples of this because it has been such a huge success; one of the reasons being that it eliminates the middleman and the extra costs, time and monopoly usually associated with middlemen. Businesses can offer their goods and services at close to cost price, maintaining an edge over other businesses that have through go through the [levelled] traditional marketing strategy: manufacturer   to   wholesaler   to   retailer   to   consumer.   An   success   story   is www.villagepottery.ca as narrated by Innovation P.E.I. (2013). Another example, mentioned by Combe (2006) is Dell's direct delivery of custom-built PCs.

Business to Business (B2B) – In its inception, business to business dealings were done using Electronic Data Interchange (EDI) where businesses exchanged business documents electronically, to facilitate business processes. B2B has been by far the most practiced ecommerce model, however, B2C is catching up. B2B facilitates transactions for goods and service between companies, allowing them to sell over the internet, and also for supply chain integration. For further texts on supply chain ecommerce integration, please read *The Frontiers Of Ebusiness Technology And Supply Chains* by Boone & Ganeshan (2007). Of course there are issues with B2B applications which include security, speed and complexity (Adewole, 2017). IST- Africa Consortium (2006) includes the following: lack of awareness; incompatibilities with technical standards; and financial barriers.

Consumer to Consumer – As already suspected, it involves consumers engaging in transactions with each other with a minimalistic portal being an intermediary between or amongst them. There are many successful examples of this model, eBay being the one that readily comes to mind. Etsy, which allows users to put up their used items and crafts for sale is also gaining headway. Craigslist, a classified ads portal was a huge success in the last decade.

Consumer to Business to Consumer – This model is similar to C2C, however, it differs in that it requires a business to provide services to facilitate interaction and exchange of goods and services. These can include passive interaction with consumers such as provision of storage, payment processing, shopping cart, security; or a more active role such as escrow services which we find in Alibaba's AliExpress™.

Business to Business to Business – This is a popular model where manufacturers of goods or service providers offer their commodities to other businesses specialized in online and ecommerce business. This takes the load off the manufacturer and allows them concentrate what they know how to do best, and also compete in cyberspace. Many Original Equipment Manufacturers (OEMs) employ such tactics. Automobile companies enter into agreements with car dealers to sell their vehicles over the internet; so also do electronics makers like Sharp and Sony, deal with large stores such as Amazon™, Walmart™ and Best Buy™.

Auction model – This model has seen success in the art and fine art industry, and also the used item category. There are always used items to sell – people will have things they no longer need but other people place value on; there are always deals on products – some individuals may get their hands on items cheaper than other do and are willing to place them on auction. Also there are always items that do not have a fixed price in the market, such as arts and crafts. The first place the owner of such item thinks of is eBay. And to be humorous, probably also the second place they think of.

The model discussed in this paper – bargain model – has similarities with the auction model. While the auction model (that is, eBay style auction, because auction has many variants) involves one seller and several buyers, that which is discussed here involves one seller and one buyer, concurrently. More of that further down the paper.

Portal model – This comprises horizontal model and vertical model. The portal is a website that aggregates various information, businesses and activities in one place. This can be information with varied interests, as in the horizontal model; or narrowed down to a particular field, offering in-depth content and services in that same field, as in the case of vertical model. Yahoo!^{TM} and MSN^{TM} are examples of horizontal model, allrecipes.com and bbcfood.com are examples of vertical models catering to fans of gastronomy and cooking. Two of which are the writer's favourite websites, by the way.

Dynamic pricing model – As the name goes, refers to when the price is never static but changing dependent on whatever factor that is being applied to it. This may be as a result of user input or it may be computer-generated. Adewole in his book entitled, *E-Business Concept & Its Applications*, gives a number of varieties of dynamic model, namely:

i.   Comparison pricing model
ii. Demand-sensitive pricing model
iii. Bartering model

Notice that what he calls bartering, is what is refered to in this paper as bargaining. In the United States, it is popularly called haggling. More on that on the 'Bargain Model Per Se' section.

2.4   Bargain model per se

Finally, we are at the *meat* of the paper! The bargain model. Bargain is a word synonymous with haggle, and with barter and negotiate. Let us take a look at several dictionaries to give us an idea of the concept. It will be best we look at their meanings in their doing form (verb).

Dictionary.com

Bargain – "to discuss the terms of a bargain; haggle; negotiate".

Barter – "to exchange in trade, as one commodity for another; trade".

Haggle – "to bargain in a petty, quibbling, and often contentious manner".

Negotiate – "to deal or bargain with another or others, as in the preparation of a treaty or contract or in preliminaries to a business deal".

Oxford Dictionary

Bargain – "Negotiate the terms and conditions of a transaction".

Barter – "Exchange (goods or services) for other goods or services without using money".

Haggle – "[*no suitable entry*]

Negotiate – "Try to reach an agreement or compromise by discussion".

Merriam-Webster Dictionary

Bargain – "[*no entry*]

Barter – "to trade by exchanging one commodity for another".

Haggle – "bargain; wrangle".

Negotiate – "to deal with (some matter or affair that requires ability for its successful handling)".

The term 'negotiate' seems to be the one that best describes what this model is about, hence the paper. However, in everyday spoken English, haggle, barter or bargain are used. In Nigerian English – if there is something called Nigerian English – bargain is the word of choice. Hence, we will refer to the idea as bargain.

Online bargain has seen very little attention – there has been more attention on online auction, especially on English auction popularized by eBay^{TM}. Bargaining model is a type of dynamic pricing. Dynamic pricing is defined by Kephart, Hanson and Greenwald in Sheng's (2004) work as "the flexible pricing strategy that could change the price of a product at any time". "Under dynamic pricing strategy, the price of a product can be changed from customer to customer, from transaction to transaction or even within a transaction" (Kannan and Kopalle, 2001) as cited by Sheng (2004).

"In an auctioning process, there are usually multiple buyers or multiple sellers participating in price negotiation" (Sheng, 2004). Citing Sheng's (2004) work, "when the number of the buyers and the number of sellers in price exchange is reduced to one, it becomes a bargaining process" (Guttman and Maes, 1998). Hence, bargains can be unilateral or multilateral. "Multilateral refers to the ability of buyer and seller agents to manage multiple simultaneous bilateral negotiations with other seller or buyer agents" (Cardoso & Oliveira, 2008).

2.5 Yihua Philip Sheng's work

Yihua Philip Sheng, a Ph. D candidate in the College of Business and Administration at Southern Illionois University published a paper titled *A Dynamic And Adaptive Bargaining Algorithm For Intelligent Selling Agents In Electronic Commerce*, in the International Journal of Computers, Systems and Signals, Vol 5, No. 1, 2004. In this paper, he wrote extensively on dynamic pricing and online bargaining per se. He observed that customers of ecommerce preferred retailing websites that offer online bargaining services. However, he also points out the fact that there is an information asymmetry between seller side and buyer side. Even tough, this paper was published 13 years ago, the situation is still true today. His paper takes a tour of market behaviour and benefits to sellers using a dynamic price change strategy using real-time bargaining information (Sheng, 2004).

In a bargaining process, a seller sets an asking price and a buyer makes an offer. The seller gradually drops price while the buyer gradually increases price until they meet at common ground. However, this is not always the case. Because bargaining is dynamic, the seller may decide to increase their price if they find that market factors favour them. Sheng's differs from the work done in this paper in that he tries to automate the process using a buyer agent and a seller agent. This automation is done using a function which takes into consideration all possible factors that could affect a bargaining process. Cardoso and Oliveira (2008) in their work titled "A Platform for Electronic Commerce with Adaptive Agents" implement a learning curve using machine learning, to not only allow the agents perform tasks without human intervention, but also to enable these agents to learn from their bargain patterns and mistakes, and make better decisions next time. The below diagram taken from Sheng's work shows how bargaining online both creates extra gain for the seller and savings for the buyer. Bother seller and buyer seem to leave the transactions more satisifed that they would have been if the product was sold and bought over a fixed price or at some sort of auction.

Figure 1 - Price change strategy (Sheng, 2004)

CHAPTER THREE

SYSTEM ANALYSIS AND DESIGN

3.1   Overview

Our analysis and design will follow the object orientation methodology. Object-oriented technology (OOT) came as a 'lifesaver' used to alleviate the software crisis that was encountered by functional development. It brought in a new era of software development way of thinking. It is "a software development technique that involves modelling software in terms of real world objects" (Korede, 2009). These objects may be tangible phenomenon, roles, interactions, systems, incidents or occurrences. There are four main areas of object-oriented technology, according to Ayo Korede (2009), viz:

i.   Object-Oriented Analysis (OOA)
ii.   Object-Oriented Design (OOD)
iii.   Object-Oriented Programming (OOP)
iv.   Object-Oriented Database (OODB)

This works make use of the first three areas, while using relational database, Entity-Relationship in Postgres for the database design and rendering.

Hence, in this section, the reader will encounter Unified Modelling Language (UML) diagrams. It is worthy to note that the system was developed using agile methodology, hence, design and development were done simultaneously. Here are the diagrams take will be looked into:

i.   Use case diagram
ii.   Activity diagram
iii.   Sequence diagram
iv.   Class diagrams
v.   Communication diagram, also known as collaboration diagram
vi.   Behaviour state diagram, also known as state diagram, or state machine
vii.   Unser interface diagram

3.2   **Requirements analysis**

3.2.1   **Requirements elicitation**

3.2.1.1 Functional requirements

Seller

- Ability to place an item up for sale
- Update item information (including description, shipping cost, quantity available, *buy now* feature)
- Delete or have an item unlisted if there are no offers
- Sets list (asking price)
- Can set reserve price
- Compose messages
- Select predefined messages
- Respond to offers
- Can activate/deactivate seller bot
- Opt out of haggling process at any time
- Block/flag a buyer
- View history of buyer interests
- View bargains currently in progress

Buyer

- Can make offer
- Can counter-offer
- Can set highest offer
- Can claim offer with *buy now* feature
- Can opt out of haggling process
- Can proceed to checkout after agreement between buyer and seller

Admin

- Block or remove a user
- Perform general ecommerce admin activities
- View all current bargains in progress

- Receive email designated to customer support and respond to these

System / Client

- Sends notifications when an offer is made
- Send notification alerts to both buyer and seller when a deal is made
- Provides input field for amount and note
- Allow listing of items for bargaining
- Close sale and make product temporarily unavailable when agreement is reached between seller and buyer
- Allow offers to be placed, and increments and decrement offers to be made as users enter new offers
- Allow multiple offers to be placed by different buyers
- Link to shopping cart API
- Allow item to be placed in shopping cart if the *buy now* feature is selected

3.2.1.2   Non-functional requirements

- Secure
- Efficient
- Reliable
- Timely
- Portable
- Appealing appearance

3.2.2   System Requirements Analysis

Requirement Analysis is defined as "the process of defining user expectations for a new software being built or modified (Teknorix Systems, 2015); it may also be referred to as Requirement Engineering".

In this section, we will attempt to analyse the requirements in order for them meet the following requirements:

- Unambiguous
- Verifiable
- Clear

- Concise
- Correct
- Complete
- Consistent
- Understandable
- Feasible (Zielczynski, 2007)
- Independent

As earlier mentioned, our prototype is a skinned down version of the business viable product. We will include only basic functional requirements for the first phase of prototyping and for demonstration purposes. These requirements are thus listed:

3.3 Use Case Analysis

Purpose

The purpose for this section is to capture the requirements for Prototype One

Actors

This section is intended for the following actors:

1. Seller
2. Duyer
3. Admin
4. System

3.3.1 Background

This system is expected to allow buyer and seller bargain (haggle) prices on an ecommerce site, just as is observed in a physical market. It is a stripped down version of the market version - Prototype Two.

Let us remember that we take into consideration the fact that this system is embedded into an ecommerce platform with ecommerce rules, serving as its containing environment. Hence, we may not include requirements which are common to ecommerce sites such as 'register, 'list products', 'set production description', and so on. It is understood that these have already been done to get to this stage.

High-level requirements

ID	Requirement	Specification	Business rule

SRS001	Login	• Only registered users should be able to log into the platform. User must login with the following credentials:
		  ○ Username
		  ○ Password
		• Access to application functionality shall be restricted by roles assigned to each user (Osemwegie, Banjoko, Otono, Chijioke-Ugwu, & Uzo, 2016). The following roles have been defined:
		  ○ Seller
		  ○ Buyer
		  ○ Admin
		• There shall be an audit trail of all activities carried out on the application.
		• It is understood that the user must already be registered to attempt login.
			Event logs on the system may not be deleted.

SRS002	Set price levels	• Seller sets the list price (asking price) and a reserve price • Buyer offer price and their own highest offer price	User must have an account and be signed in
SRS003	Interact with external ecommerce platform	The system is embedded on the ecommerce via API to edit data such as: • List products • Set product description • Integrate to shopping cart / checkout • Send messages to other users	
SRS004	Make offer and counter-offer	Users make offers and counter-offers. They can also: • Send a predefined message • Compose a note	This is only available to seller and buyer

		• Accept an offer	
		• Decline an offer	
		Admin can only accept or decline an offer on behalf of a seller/buyer.	

SRS005	Send notifications and reminders	• Admin or the system can generate a reminder if the other negotiating participant takes too long to respond
		 • System can also send reminders with time constraint settings.
		 • Logs also need to be kept of events such as:
		  o Offers
		  o Counter-offers
		  o Decline
		  o Deal
		  o Error messages	

SRS006	Send/receive second level reminder.	Also, when time remaining becomes critical, admin is alerted, which allows them to take an action such as make a telephone call.	Only the system can per such automated tasks

3.3.2   Use Case Diagram

What is a use case diagram? According to Object Management Group (as cited in Visual Paradigm, 2016), is "a kind of United Modeling Language (UML) diagram created for requirement elicitation". "It is mainly by actors, use cases and associations (connectors)" (Visual Paradigm, 2016).

Figure 2 - Use case diagram

3.3.3   Use Case

Use case is used in software development to "describe how the product will be used in specific situations" (Maxim, 2012). "Not all actors can be identified during the first iteration of requirements elicitation, but it is important to identify the primary actors before developing the use cases" (Maxim, 2012).

SRS001 - Login

Introduction

It is understood that the user must login to perform certain methods is the system. Only registered users can login with a username and password.

Actors

Seller, buyer, admin

Precondition

User must be previously registered.

Post-condition

"If the credentials supplied are (sic) valid, the user is logged onto the system, otherwise, a message is displayed 'wrong username or password'" (Osemwegie, Banjoko, Otono, Chijioke-Ugwu, & Uzo, 2016).

Basic flow

1. This use case starts when 'sign in' is clicked on the homepage to launch the sign in page.
2. The software system displays two text fields requesting for username and password to be entered.
3. The actor enters their username and password.
4. The system validates the supplied credentials, and grants access to users if correct.

Alternative flow

"If invalid credentials are keyed in by the user, the system returns a message 'Invalid username / password'" (Osemwegie et al , 2016).

Special relationship

None

Use case requirement

None

SRS002 – Set price levels

Introduction

This case shows how a user sets and edits price: Seller sets list price (also known as asking price).

Actors

Seller

Precondition

Seller must be an ecommerce account holder and be signed in to set a price.

Post-condition

Once price is set, the system registers it. Buyer may decide not to set reserve price, and just go in and bargain. Seller may also decide not to set reserve price, but must set a list price.

Basic flow

Seller

1. Seller clicks on 'set price'.
2. Seller has a field input to set, viz: List price. Integers only; Naira sign appears at the left hand side.
3. Seller clicks 'submit' and the data is registered on the database.

Alternative flow

1. The system will throw up an error message ('please set list price') when list price is not set.

Special requirement

None

Use case relationship

None

SRS003 – Interact with external ecommerce environment

Introduction

This software system is designed to be embedded on an existing ecommerce platform, hence, there needs to be quick and easy interaction with the embodying system.

Actors

Seller, buyer, admin, system

Precondition

The only precondition would be that the bargain software should be embedded on the surrounding ecommerce platform. The system should be able to have access to product information; deals (that is, agreements between seller and buyer) should be sent to shopping cart for checkout; offers made on the system should be able to be delivered to other participants using the SMTP or IRC framework of the ecommerce platform.

Post-condition

If the use case is successful, the ecommerce platform should throw a success feedback.

Basic flow

1. Actor makes a command by clicking on a button or clickable text.
2. Actor receives feedback from the external system.

Alternative flow

Specific error message is displayed pertaining to the already predefined exception.

Special relationship

None

Use case requirement

None

SRS004 – Make offer / counter-offer

Introduction

Here is the bargaining process proper, where seller or buyer can make offers while the other responds.

Actors

Seller, buyer

Precondition

1. Seller:
    a. Product and product details must have been set.
    b. Buyer must have responded to list price set by seller.
    c. Counter-offer must be lower than seller's list price.
    d. Bargain time window is set to infinity.
2. Buyer
    a. List price must already be set by seller and be viewable by the buyer.
    b. Counter-offer must be higher than buyer's previous offer, if making a second offer.
    c. Bargain time window is set to 2 hours.

Post-condition

Actor receives feedback "Your offer has been sent".

- For seller
    o 'Your offer has been sent. You can cancel the offer after 3 days of no response for the buyer.'
    o A notification will be sent by the system to the buyer.
- For buyer
    o 'Your offer has been sent. If seller does not respond within 2 hours, bargain window will be close. And seller will be penalized.'
    o A notification will be sent by the system to the seller.

Basic flow

1. Seller/Buyer sets offer amount.
2. Seller/Buyer clicks on 'Accept' in the case where the participant wants to seal a deal at the prevailing amount.
3. Seller/Buyer clicks on 'Decline' in the case where the participant wants to opt out of the negotiation process.
4. Seller/Buyer chooses a predefined message or composes one in the text box available.
5. Seller/Buyer clicks on 'Make a counter-offer'.
6. Time window is set by the system if applicable.

Alternative flow

1. Seller receives error message 'Amount must be lower than list price' if seller sets an amount equal to or greater than the list price.
2. Seller receives error message 'Amount must be lower than previous offer' if seller sets an amount greater than their previous offer.
3. Buyer receives error message 'Amount must be greater than previous offer' if buyer sets an amount than is equal to or lower than their previous offer.

Special relationship

None

Use case requirement

None

SRS005 – Send reminders

Introduction

Remember that this is an interaction-based system, where events occur and information is sent back and forth, and where the one participant must respond before the other can take an action. This means that the longer it takes a buyer or seller to respond, the less enjoyable the bargaining experience.

Therefore, it is useful to send reminders in form of text, email or phone vibration, which will remind the participant to take necessary action. The system will be responsible for sending reminders. However, admin can also step in to send reminders manually.

Actors

Admin, system

Precondition

There must be an existing offer

Post-condition

Seller/buyer will receive an email or SMS at set time.

Basic flow

At pre-set time of 1 hour 30 minutes, the system is triggered to send an email or SMS or both, depending on which channel was chosen by the customer, to remind them that their bargain activity is about to expire and they need to respond to continue the process.

Admin can manually push notifications at any time.

Alternative flow

None

Special relationship

None

Use case requirement

None

SRS006 - Send/receive second level reminder

Introduction

When the bargain time window has reached critical level, then there might be need for human intervention. Admin receives an indication that critical time limit has been reached and they can decide to place a call to the customer.

Actors

Admin

Precondition

Critical time level must have been reached.

Post-condition

All negotiations on critical time limit is displayed to admin and updated real-time. A red signal by the side of the order informs admin of the status. All concurrently logged in admin may view this table and take action.

Basic flow

1. Time allowed reached 1 hour 45 mins.
2. Bargain process turns from amber to red.
3. An agent (admin) may take responsibility by placing a call to the seller to confirm if they want to accept, reject or counter-offer.

Alternative flow

If the seller responds, the bar turns back to green

Special relationship

None

Use case requirement

None

3.4 Activity Diagram

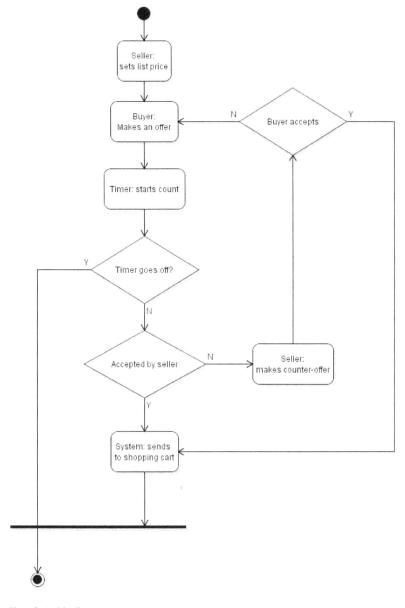

Figure 3 - Activity diagram

3.5   Class Diagram

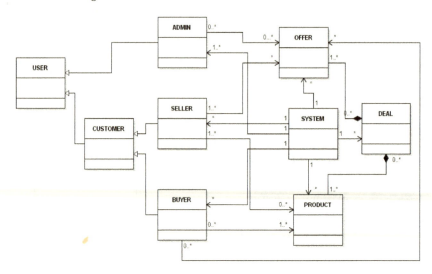

Figure 4 - Class diagram

3.5   Sequence Diagram

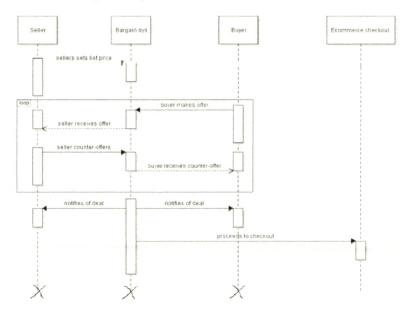

Figure 5 - Sequence diagram

3.6   Class Diagram (Detailed)

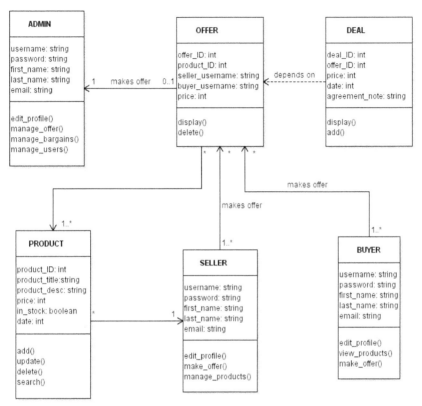

Figure 6 - Detailed class diagram

3.7   Communication diagram

Communication diagram is a type of UML interaction diagram. It is also known as collaboration diagram. According to (Luo, ?), "collaboration diagrams are equivalent to sequence diagrams. All the features of sequence diagrams are equally applicable to collaboration diagrams".

The following communication diagram is with the buyer as a perspective. These are the basic commands of a buyer communicating with the system and the unseen database.

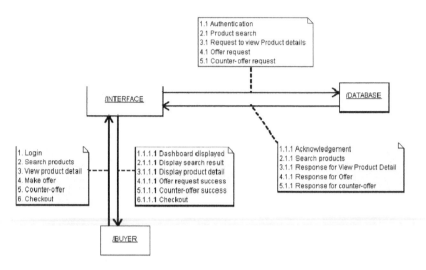

Figure 7 - Communication diagram

3.8   Behaviour State Diagram

Here below is a behaviour state diagram of the **product**. You can see from the diagram that from 'start' the product enters a state of 'listed' – this is after the seller has set a list price for the product, and it has become available to the public. The product then enters the next stage of 'active' – this is when the first offer has been made, and it can be repetitive, because offers and counter-offers can be made back and forth. Product enters a 'sold' state if an agreement has been made between buyer and seller.

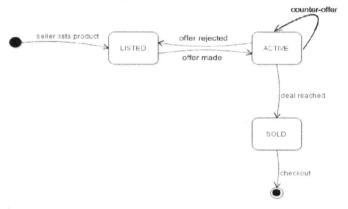

Figure 8 - State machine

3.9   E-R Diagram

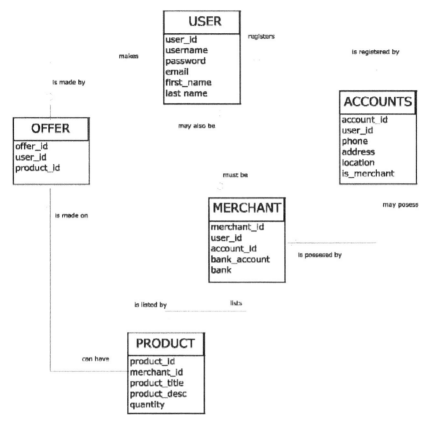

Figure 9 - E-R Diagram

3.10   Data Storage Design

Data Dictionary

Table Name User

Primary keys: User_ID, username

Description: It stores user details: Admin, seller or buyer

SN	Column name	Data type	Size	Constraint	Description
1	User_ID	Integer	25	Primary key	Computer-generated
2	Username	Varchar	25	Primary key	It is referenced to the Login table
3	FirstName	Varchar	25	Not null	It stores user's first name
4	LastName	Varchar	25	Not null	It stores user's last name
5	Gender	Varchar	6	Not null	Checks whether the user is male or female
6	Address	Varchar	100	Not null	It stores user's address
7	Country	Varchar	30	Foreign key	It references the Country table
8	State	Varchar	30	Foreign key	It references the State table
9	City	Varchar	30	Foreign key	It references the City table
10	Email	Varchar	40	Not null	It stores user's email
11	Phone	Integer	15	Not null	It stores user's telephone number
12	Photo	Varchar	100	Not null	It stores user's personal photo
13	Password	Varchar	25	Not null	It stores users password
14	Type	Varchar	7	Not null	Checks whether user is admin or not

Table Name Product

Primary keys: Product_ID

Foreign key: Username

Description: It stores data of products uploaded by seller

SN	Column name	Data type	Size	Constraint	Description
1	Product_ID	Integer	25	Primary key	It stores computer-generated product_ID
2	Product title	char	100	Not null	It stores product name and title
3	Username	Varchar	25	Foreign key	It references the User_Master table
4	Description	Varchar	250	Not null	It stores product description
5	Status	Boolean	1	Not null	Checks if product is open to offers or not
6	Photo	Varchar	100	Not null	Stores photo of the product
7	List_Date	Datetime	-	Not null	It stores date and time product was made available
8	Last_Offer_Date	Datetime	-	Not null	It store date and time last offer was made

Table Name Offer

Primary keys: Offer_ID

Foreign key: Product_ID, Username

Description: It stores offer details

SN	Column name	Data type	Size	Constraint	Description
1	Offer_ID	Integer	100	Primary key	It stores ID of offer
2	Product_ID	Integer	25	Foreign key	ID of product from Product_Master
3	Username	Varchar	25	Foreign key	It references the User_Master table

4	Offer_Date	Datetime	-	Not null	It stores time and date of offer
5	Bid_Price	Double	15	Not null	It stores bid price of products
6	Is deal?	Boolean	-	Not null	It stores if offer has been confirmed as deal or not

Table Name: Merchant

Primary keys:

Foreign key:

Description: It stores information of merchants

SN	Column name	Data type	Size	Constraint	Description
1	Product_ID	Integer	25	Foreign key	It links to product table
2	Business name	Varchar	25	Not null	It stores first name of customer
3	Bank account	Integer	10	Not null	It stores bank account number
4	Bank name	String	25	Not null	It stores bank name

3.11   User Interface

Below are user interface diagrams for seller and buyer

Seller UI

Figure 10 – User Interface Login

Figure 11 – User Interface - My products

Figure 12- User Interface - Set price

Figure 13 - User Interface - New offer

For the buyer...

Login (same as for seller)

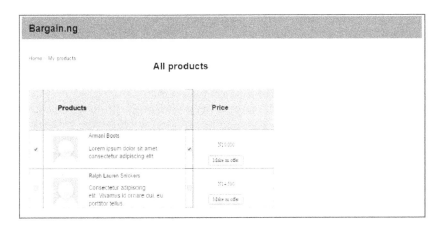

Figure 14 - User Interface - All products

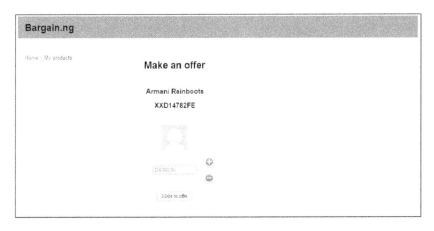

Figure 15 - User Interface - Make an offer

New offer (same as for seller)

CHAPTER FOUR

IMPLEMENTATION

4.1   **Introduction**

According to ITL Education Solutions Limited, as cited by (Jubril, 2012), hardware refers to "all physical part of a computer" system. It includes all the components that you can touch and feel. Think of matter – anything that has weight and occupies space – hardware can be understood with that analogy. It includes the central processing unit and its components, the monitor, the keyboard, mouse, printer, scanner and any other peripheral component.

Because this is a web app hosted entirely in the cloud, hardware requirements will not be demanding. Furthermore, the idea is to make the commercial version accessible to the common Nigeria, so backward support for old hardware and software will be taken into consideration.

The minimum hardware requirements for this system:

  i.   256MB RAM
  ii.   5GB hard disk space
  iii. A keyboard
  iv.   A mouse
  v.   A monitor

As earlier mentioned, hardware specifications may go even lower than this, as long as it can render the minimum software requirement.

Software

Software are written instruction which put computer hardware to work. They are written instructions that perform required tasks. According George Reynolds as cited by (Jubril, 2012), they govern the operations of a computer. We have three types of software:

  1. System software – These are those programs that built specifically to allow a system run itself. In the case of Windows, all system software end in .sys.

2. Application software – These are software that are useful on a computer. They often perform a certain task or set of tasks. They usually designed for a specific purpose. They may come preinstalled on a computer or download separately. Examples include scientific calculator, CorelDraw, Adobe Photoshop.

3. Software packages – These are a group of software that are required to perform similar tasks or a wide variety of tasks. These software are package together and sold by the developer. They come in suites or as extensions. Examples include Adobe Suite, Microsoft Office Suite.

According to The Django Project Website (2017), "Django is a high-level Python Web framework that encourages rapid development and clean, pragmatic design". They claim that it "takes care of much of the hassle of Web development, so you can focus on writing your app without needing to reinvent the wheel". And quite rightly so!

Python was the main operating programming language of this system. This system is a web app, meaning that it employs typical web languages to achieve its overall functionality, look and feel. HTML5 is the web markup language, employing CSS 3, PYTHON and Postgres for database functions. Why was Postgres chosen as the database language of choice? Here are a few reasons:

i. It is ubiquitous
ii. It is easy to use
iii. It has a multi-file handling system (Jubril, 2012)
iv. It has a good data storage capability

Software requirements

The following are needed to properly render the web application.

i. Any computer or mobile operating system from year 2000 and later
ii. A web browser, desirably Chrome no earlier than year 2012
iii. Cookies turn on
iv. An internet connection

4.2　　　　Software components

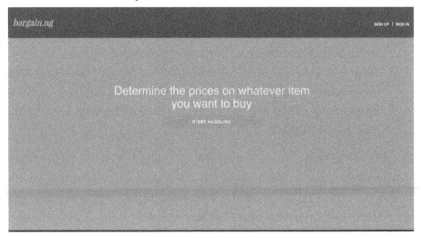

Figure 16 - Home page

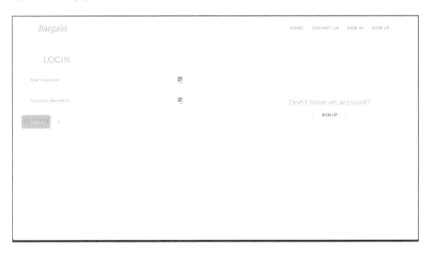

Figure 17 - Login page

37

Figure 18 - Admin page

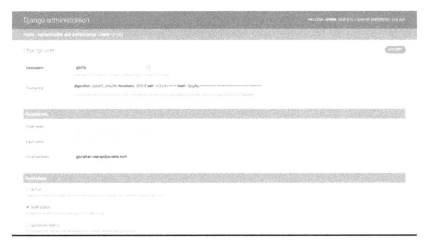

Figure 19 - Admin page - User profile

4.3   Testing

Testing was done concurrently as the system is being built, inline with agile development. Programmers write the initial codes to fulfil the design specifications; The codes are the *refactored* to make sure that they are more efficient.

Some test scripts:

Test question	Yes	No
Were admin, seller and buyer able to login?	*	
Was seller able to list prices?	*	
Was buyer able to make an offer?	*	
Was seller able to counter-offer?	*	
Did the timer (CronJob) activate and go off at the set time?	*	
Did buyer/seller get notification each time they received a counter-offer?	*	
Was the user able to navigate through easily on the entire site?	*	
When a deal was reached, was the instance update and data stored in the database?	*	

CHAPTER FIVE

CONCLUSION AND RECOMMENDATION

5.1   Summary

There are many ways to cash in on ecommerce and its reward. There is such wide information asymmetry, yes, even a massive digital divide in information technology in Nigeria. Depending on how it is exploited, it may catapult some to instant stardom and affluence or may even impoverish the already poor. It is also possible that the scene becomes a chaos if not well managed. The government needs to step and assist the citizens in ways the United States involved herself during the early development of information technology and continues to intervene positively in research, finance, education, execution of rules and regulations, as well as enforcing these laws. Nigeria as a country certain should not lag behind. Ecommerce is certainly an avenue Nigeria can pose herself as a major player, owing to the population and the growth of the economy.

5.2   Advantages and Opportunities

Why bother designing such a system anyway?

- It increases participation at an unprecedented level – Interaction, or more specifically, user participation, is what drives online businesses. It is the new currency, almost as, or if not more valuable than storage space.

- More monetization opportunities by offering premium seller/buyer bots with more advanced AI technology.

- The buyer is concerned with satisfaction, in other words, if the buyer gets 100% customer satisfaction for buying a product at a particular price, then that is the whole essence of a successful trade. Please note that price is not the only currency in a bargain process. Also note that, earlier in the paper, it was proven by Sheng (2004) that the buyer most times also gets products below the price they were actually willing to pay for it.

- Bargaining process allows buyer to get to know the product better before actually buying. This means that the buyer is completely satisfied with product and the offer before parting with their money. This means 100% customer satisfaction. This also means that the customer will most likely visit the market place again and again, or even visit the particular seller.

- It wraps up current customer behaviour in online price comparison search engines, discount requesting, and coupon craze in the online shopping arena. Online shoppers want discounts, they want the lowest price for an air fare, they want the lowest price for a PlayStation 4. They want discounts coupons, use loyalty cards and redeem gifts offered by stores, all in an effort to buy products at a lower price than is being advertised. Why not convert these expectations into the well-known and loved bargain style flea market shopping?

- Flexibility – Why have a static price, when you can take advantage of dynamic pricing and charge more/less when marketing conditions favour you? Virgillito (2016) puts it this way, "This kind of pricing flexibility results in prices that can be responsive to a variety of market conditions, and this is good for you and your customers". Virgillito, in the same paper sums it up with this figures below:

 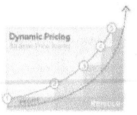

Figure 20 - Dynamic pricing (source: Virgillito, 2016)

5.3   Problems Encountered

The system developed is far from finished work, hence many problems were immediately identified.

- It takes a longer time to close a sale – This is obvious and may be bad business to investors that want to see deals closed in record time.

- It can be exhausting for the participants – Because negotiations can go back and forth several dozen times and still a compromise may not be reached.

- It may not be suited to items of low price points – It may seem like a complete waste of time for products of little value. Amazon^{TM} notices this challenge, this makes them include a constraint which only allows users to haggle on products $100 and above (Weise, 2014).

5.4   Recommendations

- In order to simplify the bargain model's complexity "simulation is the preferred method in the cases where mathematical reasoning and modelling are very complicated or even impossible" (Sheng, 2004).
- User constraints should definitely be introduced, constraints that restricts the buyer from submitting a ridiculously low amount, using the seller's cost price as a threshold.
- To enhance user experience, each time a negotiation fails, the system may recommend sellers of similar products. This will ensure that the buyer maintain interest in the product and on the ecommerce site.
- The developer may introduce multimedia to render product information, since the buyer spends more time getting to know the product. The more enjoyable the experience, the more likely the buyer is to come back, stay longer on the web site, or interact more with the site. This takes a proportion of the buyer's valuable attention from social media, which seems to be getting all the attention.

5.5   Conclusion

The paper is focused on a bargain ecommerce application. Object-oriented analysis and design was used to achieve the aim of building a working bargain software based on the web. Languages used were Python, HTML, JavaScript and SQL. Frameworks used were SASS for CSS and Django for Python. The database used was Postgres. The ecommerce site was hosted on Heroku^{TM}.

The ecommerce model known as the *bargain model*, which simulates negotiating behaviour between sellers and buyers in African, South American and Asian flea markets has been studied throughout this paper, and work by then Ph. D student, Yihua Sheng, was specifically highlighted, to show the potential of the concept.

Is the ecommerce bargain model a dark horse? Will the bargain model be the next cyberspace mega-success? Will the writer be the first to develop the first valuable system on the concept? The year 2022 should answer those questions conveniently.

REFERENCES

Adesanya, M.O., (2015) *Mobile Order Management System For Restaurants*. Lagos: University of Lagos.

Adewole, A.P., (2017) *E-Business Concept & Its Applications*. Lagos: University of Lagos.

Amadi, P.O., (2017) *Design And Implementation Of An Online Shopping Mall (A Case Study of Easyday Online Shopping Mall, Lagos State)*. Lagos: University of Lagos.

Azeez, N.A., (2016) *Basic Theory, Principles And Practices In Information Technology*. Lagos: University of Lagos.

Boone, T. & Ganeshan, R., (2007) The frontiers of eBusiness technology and supply chains. *Journal of Operations Management*, pp.1195–98.

Cardoso, E.L. & Oliveira, E., (2008) *A Platform for Electronic Commerce with Adaptive Agents*. Porto: Universidade do Porto.

Chaffey, D., (2009) *E-business And E-commerce Management - Strategy, Implementation And Practice*. Essex: Pearson Education Limited.

Combe, C., (2006) *Introduction To E-Business Management And Strategy*. Massachussetts: Elsevier 1Linacre House.

CSC2507 - Conceptual Modelling - Object-Oriented Analysis.

Fleck, D., ? *Activity Diagrams*.

Huang, G., (2009) Posted Price and Haggling in the Used Car Market. pp.1-48.

Innovation P.E.I., (2013) *How You Can Profit From E-Business - An Introductory Handbook*. Innovation P.E.I.

IST- Africa Consortium, (2006) *eBusiness - Case Studies*. IST- Africa Consortium.

Joan, Adams, P., Baker, B. & Charlie, C., (2004) *Software Requirements Specification - Web Publishing System v1.0.*

Jubril, M.B., (2012) *Implementating Ecommerce For Good Customer Service*. Lagos: University of Lagos.

Kodali, S., (2007) *The Design And Implementation Of An E-Commerce Site For Online Book Sales*. Indiana: Indiana University South Bend.

Korede, A.C., (2009) *Information Systems and Technologies*. Ogun State: Covenant University, Ota.

Lecture 1 - Chapter 5 – System Modeling.

Lewis, J., (2009) *Haggling on your mobile - BBC previews new ECS research*. [Online] Available at: HYPERLINK "http://www.iam.ecs.soton.ac.uk/news/2493" http://www.iam.ecs.soton.ac.uk/news/2493 [Accessed 20 November 2017].

Luo, Y., ? *EEL5881 Software Engineering I - UML Lecture*.

Maxim, B., (2012) *Requirements Analysis*. [Online] Available at: HYPERLINK "https://www.slideshare.net/asimnawaz54/requirements-analysis-15191479" https://www.slideshare.net/asimnawaz54/requirements-analysis-15191479 [Accessed 23 November 2017].

Mind Tools Content Team, ? *Business Requirements Analysis*. [Online] Available at: HYPERLINK "https://www.mindtools.com/pages/article/newPPM_77.htm" https://www.mindtools.com/pages/article/newPPM_77.htm [Accessed 23 November 2017].

Moertini, V.S., Suhok, Heriyanto, S. & Nugroho, C.D., (2014) Requirement Analysis Method Of Website Development For Small-Medium Enterprise, Case Study: Indonesia. *International Journal of Software Engineering & Applications (IJSEA)*, pp.12-28.

Osemwegie, I.M. et al., (2016) *System Requirement Specification - Students' Result Management System*. Lagos.

Osemwegie, I.M. et al., (2016) *Students' Result Management System - Function-Oriented Design & Object-Oriented Design*. Lagos.

Osobov, A., (2012) *Class and Sequence Diagrams*. CSE 403.

Pande, U.S. & Shukl, S., (2011) *E-commerce And Mobile Commerce Technologies*. New Delhi: S. Chand & Company Ltd.

Peachey, K., (2009) *I'll give you a tenner for that*. [Online] Available at: HYPERLINK "http://news.bbc.co.uk/2/hi/business/8008865.stm" http://news.bbc.co.uk/2/hi/business/8008865.stm [Accessed 20 November 2017].

Pricedex Software Inc., (2006) *Dynamic Pricing: Paradigm or Paradox?* Pricedex Software Inc.

Sheng, Y.P., (2004) A Dynamic And Adaptive Bargaining Algorithm For Intelligent Selling Agents In Electronic Commerce. *International Journal of Computers, Systems and Signals, Vol 5*, pp.43-55.

Teknorix Systems, (2015) *Requirements Analysis.* [Online] Available at: HYPERLINK "http://www.teknorix.com/methodology/requirements-analysis" http://www.teknorix.com/methodology/requirements-analysis [Accessed 26 November 2017].

The Django Project, (2017) *The Django Project.* [Online] Available at: HYPERLINK "https://www.djangoproject.com/" https://www.djangoproject.com/ [Accessed 6 December 2017].

Virgillito, D., (2016) *Dynamic Pricing: The Art and Black Magic of Situational Pricing.* [Online] Available at: HYPERLINK "https://www.shopify.com/enterprise/102104006-dynamic-pricing-the-art-and-black-magic-of-situational-pricing" https://www.shopify.com/enterprise/102104006-dynamic-pricing-the-art-and-black-magic-of-situational-pricing [Accessed 20 November 2017].

Visual Paradigm, (2016) *How to Write Effective Use Cases?* [Online] Available at: HYPERLINK "https://www.visual-paradigm.com/tutorials/writingeffectiveusecase.jsp" https://www.visual-paradigm.com/tutorials/writingeffectiveusecase.jsp [Accessed 26 November 2017].

Waal, P.d., (2014) Lecture 1 - Introduction to e-business and e-commerce. *E-commerce,* 10 November. pp.1-44.

Wang, J., (2016) Object Oriented Analysis Methodology. *MSIS488 Information Systems Analysis.*

Weise, E., (2014) *Now you can haggle on Amazon.* [Online] Available at: HYPERLINK "https://www.usatoday.com/story/tech/2014/12/09/bargaining-dicker-amazon-make-an-offer-haggle/20021265/" https://www.usatoday.com/story/tech/2014/12/09/bargaining-dicker-amazon-make-an-offer-haggle/20021265/ [Accessed 20 November 2017].

Wikipedia, (2017) *Django (web framework).* [Online] Available at: HYPERLINK "https://en.wikipedia.org/wiki/Django_(web_framework)" https://en.wikipedia.org/wiki/Django_(web_framework) [Accessed 5 December 2017].

Zielczynski, P., (2007) *Requirements Management Using IBM® Rational® RequisitePro®.* IBM Press. Available at: HYPERLINK "http://www.informit.com/articles/article.aspx?p=1152528&seqNum=4" http://www.informit.com/articles/article.aspx?p=1152528&seqNum=4 [accessed 26 November 2017].

Θεοφάνης, Δ. & Λογισμικού, Τ., (2008) *Software Requirements Specification For iTest.*

YOUR KNOWLEDGE HAS VALUE

- We will publish your bachelor's and
  master's thesis, essays and papers

- Your own eBook and book -
  sold worldwide in all relevant shops

- Earn money with each sale

Upload your text at www.GRIN.com
and publish for free

GRIN

www.ingramcontent.com/pod-product-compliance
Lightning Source LLC
La Vergne TN
LVHW092354060326
832902LV00008B/1038